D0118928

GALAXY OF SUPERSTARS

CHELSEA HOUSE PUBLISHERS

GALAXY OF SUPERSTARS

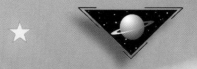

Drew Barrymore

John Bankston

CHELSEA HOUSE PUBLISHERS
Philadelphia

Frontis: At age 25, Drew Barrymore reaps the benefits of a long struggle back to stardom. Her triumph over depression and addiction made her return to film not just a dream, but a reality.

CHELSEA HOUSE PUBLISHERS
Editor in Chief: Sally Cheney
Director of Production: Kim Shinners
Creative Manager: Takeshi Takahashi
Manufacturing Manager: Diann Grasse

Staff for DREW BARRYMORE
Associate Editor: Ben Kim
Picture Researcher: Jane Sanders
Production Assistant: Jaimie Winkler
Series Designer: Takeshi Takahashi
Cover Designer: Terry Mallon
Layout: 21st Century Publishing and Communications, Inc.

© 2002 by Chelsea House Publishers, a subsidiary of
Haights Cross Communications. All rights reserved.
Printed and bound in the United States of America.

The Chelsea House World Wide Web address is
http://www.chelseahouse.com

First Printing

1 3 5 7 9 8 6 4 2

Library of Congress Cataloging-in-Publication Data

Bankston, John, 1974–
  Drew Barrymore / John Bankston.
    p. cm. — (Galaxy of superstars)
Summary: A biography of the young star of the movie "E.T." who survived
her troubled early years and has gone on to become a successful actress
and movie producer.
Includes bibliographical references and index.
  ISBN 0-7910-6772-6
  1. Barrymore, Drew—Juvenile literature. 2. Motion picture actors and
actresses—United States—Biography—Juvenile literature. [1. Barrymore,
Drew. 2. Actors and actresses. 3. Women—Biography.] I. Title. II. Series.
PN2287.B29 B36 2002
791.43'028'092—dc21
                                    2002000346

CONTENTS

A NEW ANGEL

The wrap party at Drew Barrymore's Beverly Hills home was a celebration. It's normal to have a party after the final day of filming when a movie is "wrapped," or done shooting. The process of making a movie—known as the "shoot"—can last several months and cost tens of millions of dollars. By the time it's over, the dedicated professionals who have devoted 12- to 16-hour days to the movie might be exhausted, but they're also ready for a party.

Most of the lucky people who attended the spring 2000 wrap party for *Charlie's Angels* believed that it was the best wrap party ever. Over 1,000 people arrived at the 5,000-square-foot manse in the City of Angels' famous 90210 zip code. As both the star and producer of the movie, Drew knew firsthand how difficult the shoot had been, and she felt that she owed the cast and crew a memorable evening.

When they arrived, the guests found four bars and plenty of food. One room featured canvases and paint and some guests spent part of their evening creating works of art. Others devoted an hour or two to the game room and its fierce air hockey competition. Still, the most popular room was the one showing reruns of the television show the movie was based on.

Drew accepts the Hasty Pudding Pot Award honoring her as the "Woman of the Year." Her career seems to be on the rise, made all the more amazing by her problems in the late '80s and her struggle to overcome them.

"I've had parties before where I've tried to screen stuff," Drew told *Premiere* magazine. "And people at parties just don't have the attention span." At this party, guests actually watched entire episodes, ignoring the rest of the festivities. Considering most of them had already spent over 100 days of their life devoted to the movie based on the same television show, their interest was surprising. But then for many, the popularity of the original show was also a surprise.

The movie *Charlie's Angels* was an update of the popular 1970s television show. From the moment it debuted in September 1976, half of the television sets in the United States were tuned in to the adventures of three good-looking female detectives played by Farrah Fawcett, Kate Jackson, and Jaclyn Smith.

Although the series premiered the year after Drew was born, she'd seen enough reruns to believe it would make an interesting movie. For her, the quarter-century distance made the show cool again. She thought it would be a good project for her production company, Flower Films.

Taking on *Charlie's Angels* meant producing a film that required expensive stunt work, special effects, and a ballooning budget which eventually reached over $80 million—twice as high as for her last film. "We kind of skipped steps two, three, and four and went to five," Drew admitted to *Premiere*.

Drew knew she could handle the responsibility. She began by making changes to the television show's story. Although the detectives were pretty, Drew felt the original's success wasn't just about how the women looked. To Drew, *Charlie's Angels'* strength was its focus on three independent women who could handle themselves. Although she planned to keep the original's basic plot, along with the various skimpy outfits the detectives wore as part of their crime-solving duties, Drew made one major change.

In Drew Barrymore's movie, the detectives wouldn't use guns.

"I know this is going to sound strange, but I think it's cowardly to flick a finger and kill someone," Drew told the *Entertainment Weekly* website. "I'm much more interested in. . . . how different the world would be if people had to kill each other with their hands."

Instead of guns, the actresses would use a combination of kung fu and street-fighting moves. To make their marital arts seem realistic, Drew and the actresses she hired—Lucy Liu and Cameron Diaz—trained for months before filming began. Relying on kung fu master Cheung-Yan Yuen—who prepared Keanu Reeves for *The Matrix*—and his nine assistants, the three young women worked out eight hours a day.

Although her costars were very involved with the project, Drew knew she was the one with the most responsibility. As the film's producer, if the movie failed, she'd get most of the blame. Although in every interview Drew expressed confidence in the film's success, negative articles about the movie were written before an inch of celluloid was exposed. The articles criticized the budget, the story, and especially the inexperienced director. The movie's director, McG (Joseph McGinty Nichol), a native Californian, was still in his twenties when the filming began. He'd never directed a feature film before, just commercials and videos for bands like Sugar Ray and Smash Mouth. In his earlier work, the job was usually over in a day or two. The *Charlie's Angels* shoot would last 100 days.

An even bigger question was whether audiences would go see a movie without male stars. Cameron Diaz, Lucy Liu, and Drew Barrymore were all

Drew Barrymore produced the film *Charlie's Angels* and threw a gigantic party for the cast and crew at her home. Consistent with Drew's personality, her party was quirky and a little different from the norm. She put painting supplies in one room so her guests could create art.

famous, but were their names so well known that *Charlie's Angels* would be number one at the box office for its opening weekend? Stories about young women with fighting skills had been successful—but only on television. Although programs like *Buffy the Vampire Slayer*, and the more recent *Dark Angel*, were hits, the idea hadn't worked in a movie—yet.

Drew faced more than just questions about the movie's subject. Many articles focused on the production itself. Articles about movies in production often deal with the problems on the set. Sometimes these reports helped sink already troubled pictures. By the time *Charlie's Angels* began filming, reports from the set included vivid descriptions of fights with the director, budget problems, and conflicts involving comedic actor Bill Murray, who had taken on the part of Bosley.

The battles between the women got the most attention. To the film's stars, the tone of many of the articles seemed blatantly sexist with words like "cat fight" used to describe the young actresses' disagreements. In an interview with *Microsoft News*, Cameron Diaz responded to the rumored fighting by saying, "I don't have any catty women in my life. I don't have room for jealousy. It was a dream being with these two girls."

When the movie was about to be released, the three lead actresses met with many reporters and photographers and held hands and smiled. Drew had over 15 years of experience looking positive before the press, despite her life's challenges.

Drew was only seven years old, when magazines like *People* and *US* devoted articles to her life and her scene-stealing performance in *E.T. The Extra-Terrestrial*. She was still in grade school when supermarket tabloids exposed the out-of-control nightclub partying that almost destroyed her career. Nearly every one of the publications mentioned her background as a member of a family that began acting professionally when the Civil War was still raging.

The legacy haunted Drew. Her father—John Barrymore Jr.—had destroyed a promising acting career by drinking and using drugs. As she approached her teen years, it looked like Drew would do the same thing. It would take the talented child star a great deal of effort to keep from winding up like her famous relatives. In many ways the journey prepared Drew for the challenges of the success that was yet to come.

2

THE PERFECT SCREAM

The room was crawling with babies: fat babies, skinny babies, girl and boy babies, crying babies. Although every one of them was less than a year old, they were all professional actors. It was an audition for a commercial for Gainesburgers dog food, and each of the infants spent a moment or two playing with the commercial's other star, a puppy. The casting director watched to see how they interacted with the tiny animal.

The babies didn't really have to act of course. All they needed to do was not cry, and not hurt the puppy. When Drew Barrymore's turn came, her mother Jaid watched nervously. The audition hadn't been her idea. She'd been talked into it by a children's agent, someone whose job was finding commercial and theatrical acting work for kids.

Drew was only 11 months old, a tow-headed baby with the type of winning smile and natural personality agents loved. When her name was called, her mother brought her over and the little girl began playing with the puppy.

The puppy bit her. Everyone in the room froze. They waited for the baby to cry, for the mother to threaten a lawsuit. Instead the girl looked at the puppy and giggled.

Young Drew started acting in commercials before her first birthday. Drew had a lucky streak in acting; she landed most of her auditions and won the eye of Steven Spielberg.

Drew Barrymore got the job.

It would be the first of many. Drew was a natural talent, but then "nature," or genetics, had as much to do with her future success as luck or timing.

Her mother, Ildyko Jaid Mako first met actor John Drew Barrymore Jr. a decade before on a Hollywood set. By the time they were dating, in the early 1970s, their relationship was, by both of their accounts, volatile—and even occasionally violent. John was an alcoholic and drug addict who had gone from roles in feature films like *The Sundowners* and *Never Love a Stranger* to being completely broke. Jaid was a dark-hairded Hungarian beauty who had arrived in Los Angeles with the same dreams of stardom shared by the dozens of young starlets who came to the city every day. Like most of them, she supported herself by waiting tables. Occasionally she earned a small part in a small movie and did some modeling.

When her daughter, Drew Blythe Barrymore, was born on February 22, 1975, Jaid's life was forever changed. The child arrived at Brotman Memorial Hospital in Culver City, California, a gritty section of West Los Angeles that once served as the location for many silent films in the early 1900s.

By the time Drew was born, Jaid's marriage to John was already disintegrating. She wanted her child to grow up in a healthier environment than one with a father who had a drinking problem and little else. Jaid moved into a one-bedroom duplex in West Hollywood, an eclectic neighborhood of Russian immigrants, gays, and rock clubs. She continued to waitress and audition.

In many ways, just looking for acting work is

a full-time job. Aspiring actors regularly update their headshots, or glossy photographs of their face, and send them to casting agencies. They go out on readings, take acting classes, and meet with casting directors. Between looking for an acting job and waitressing, Jaid had very little extra time for baby Drew and relied on a series of baby sitters. John was rarely around to help.

In many ways, despite her semi-famous father and aspiring actress mother, Drew's life wasn't very different from many kids with single parents. Money and child care was always a problem. Jaid was often tired and stressed. Still, Drew was a happy child, and even as a baby was very expressive. Several of Jaid's friends told her Drew was perfect for commercials.

Jaid already faced enough rejection in the entertainment industry to believe it would be a terrible life for her daughter. Like all performers, child actors face rejection daily. It is hard for even adults not to sometimes take it personally. Kids trying out for parts are often told they're "too short, too tall, too young, too old."

Although Jaid wanted to shelter her daughter, a friend sent Drew's picture to a children's agent. The agent saw potential in the photograph and pleaded with Jaid to at least take Drew on a few auditions. At first she refused, but the agent was persistent.

Jaid eventually agreed to take Drew to the audition for the dog food commercial. It was for a national advertisement that would air across the country and could mean tens of thousands of dollars.

It was Drew's first audition—but it also became her first job.

While many parents might have followed up

their child's success with round after round of auditions, Jaid was reluctant. She continued to waitress and look for her own acting jobs. By law, most of Drew's money was placed in trust—she wouldn't have access to it until she was an adult, so the money from the ad didn't change their life.

Drew didn't work again for almost two years, but again a friend of Jaid got Drew involved. Stuart Margolin was directing his first movie, *Suddenly Love*. He called Jaid because he needed a toddler to play star Cindy Williams's child. Drew had to play a boy! They cut her hair short and she had the part.

Although Jaid remained protective, she slowly allowed Drew to audition more. The first four commercials Drew went out for, she got. In an industry where even successful actors rarely get one job from twenty or thirty auditions, this type of early success was unheard of. Drew was also cast in her first feature film, the movie *Altered States*. This scary film was about a sensory deprivation tank and a man who abuses mind-altering drugs.

Despite the excitement of earning her first movie part, Drew was still a little kid—just four years old, and attending preschool. However, Drew was also slowly taking on the life of a professional actress. She had sessions with photographers. She went to auditions and commercial casting calls. She did ads for products such as Kellogg's Rice Krispies. But most important for her future career, she read for Steven Spielberg.

In 1981, Steven Spielberg was probably the hottest director in Hollywood. His films *Jaws*, *Close Encounters*, and *Raiders of the Lost Ark* were very popular. He directed his first feature film when he was only 22; he was in his thirties when he began casting sessions for a new horror film: *Poltergeist*. The movie was about a family who moves into a suburban house that is inhabited by ghosts. Drew auditioned for the part of the youngest daughter who is abducted by the spirits. As part of her audition, little Drew was asked to scream. Drew didn't get the part, but Spielberg remembered her scream.

Just one year before, he'd been in North Africa shooting the movie *Raiders of the Lost Ark*. Spielberg had felt very lonely, being away from his girlfriend and his family. Spielberg imagined what it would be like to have a perfect friend who would be there for him no matter what happened. He decided the perfect friend might be a creature from outer space. Spielberg told the idea about a friend from outer space to the wife of *Raiders* star Harrison Ford, Melissa Mathison. Mathison wrote movies for a living, and after hearing Spielberg's idea, decided to write the script. The movie was called *E.T. The Extra-Terrestrial*, about a 10-year-old boy named Elliot who discovers an alien in his backyard and brings him home.

After Spielberg returned to Los Angeles, he quickly became involved with two projects that featured children. The first was *Poltergeist*. The second was *E.T.*

As he began interviewing young actresses for the part of Gertie, Elliot's younger sister, Spielberg remembered the girl with the terrific scream. He had Drew read for the part.

Auditioning for a Steven Spielberg movie isn't like auditioning for any other picture. Spielberg felt it was important to get to know the actors, especially kids. Instead of just asking them to

Drew accepts a People's Choice Award for *ET: The Extra-Terrestrial* with co-stars Henry Thomas and Robert Macnaughton. The hit movie made Drew an instant star.

read from the script, he'd also ask them all kinds of questions. Today, this type of audition process is called "a Spielberg interview."

In the summer of 1981, six-year-old Drew came in for the Spielberg interview. Drew told the director she was in a punk rock band called the Purple People Eaters. In her autobiography, *Little Girl Lost*, Drew remembered telling Spielberg, "I sing lead. We play the clubs on weekends, you know, Madam Wong's, the Troubadour, the Roxy. Stuff like that."

Spielberg was enchanted. Drew managed to seem like a little kid and a grownup at the same time. She was bright, funny, and self-assured. Then Spielberg had her do one more thing—he had her scream. She did, and she got the part.

When Drew's mother came in, she told Spielberg her daughter had made up the story about the punk rock band. He didn't mind. He knew it meant the young actress wouldn't have any trouble pretending the alien in *E.T.* was real.

3

NEWLY FAMOUS

Drew Barrymore's life could be difficult. She loved her mother, Jaid. She even loved her father, although he wasn't around very often and acted strangely when he was. Still, the first time she felt like part of a real family was on a movie set.

The production of a major motion picture creates its own world. Trailers—fancy mobile homes—are provided for the stars. Children no longer have to worry about going to school every day as a tutor provides three hours of classroom instruction. Best of all, the craft services table offers endless quantities of cookies, candy, and soda.

Making a movie requires long hours. Although by law children can't work as much as the adults, there's a feeling on most movie sets of everyone pulling together for a common goal. Spending 12 or 16 hours a day with one group of people for several months usually creates a close, family-like atmosphere. For Drew, it felt like she was finally home.

Steven Spielberg's vision for *E.T. The Extra-Terrestrial* required "suspension of disbelief." This means while the audience knew the alien, "E.T.," wasn't real, the art of moviemaking would help them believe otherwise. For this to

---

Drew found the spotlight at an early age but also unfortunately found the partying lifestyle to her liking. Here she socializes with Stephen Pearcy of the '80s rock group Ratt.

work, the actors had to be convincing, especially the children. The acting required the three young cast members—Henry Thomas, who played Elliot; Robert MacNaughton, who played his older brother, Michael; and Drew who played the little sister, Gertie—to convince everyone E.T. was real.

That wasn't difficult for Drew. Just as many kids her age are able to pretend their dolls or stuffed animals are real, Drew was able to pretend that "E.T." was like a special friend. To everyone else in the cast and crew, E.T. was little more than a very expensive rubber toy, but to Drew he was almost human.

Leaving *E.T.* was only part of the reason the last day of filming was the hardest. Mainly it was because once the picture wrapped, Drew had to say good-bye to the director, Steven Spielberg, who had become like a substitute father for the girl.

Soon after the very emotional last day, Drew returned to regular life. Going back to the "real world" wasn't easy. When she returned to school, there were many ways that Drew felt like she didn't fit in. She was used to being around adults. Kids her own age were harder to deal with.

After Drew finished working on *E.T.*, her life improved financially. Although most of the income she earned from the movie was placed in trust, the Barrymore's lives were changed by what was left over. Money was no longer tight. Still, Jaid was very busy. Drew's mother finally had an acting job. *Night Shift* was directed by Ron Howard and starred Henry Winkler. Both men were former television actors from the show *Happy Days*. Jaid's role in the film was very small, but her days on the set were very long. Once when Drew got sick with pneumonia, her mother had to stay and work.

Drew felt abandoned. She also missed acting. She began to have problems at Fountain Day School, where she was in the first grade. She didn't get along with her classmates. When *E.T.* was released, her conflicts became even worse.

Two of Steven Spielberg's films were coming out during the summer of 1982. Most media attention was focused on the one he had written, *Poltergeist*. Directed by Tobe Hooper, who had gained fame by directing the low-budget horror classic *Texas Chainsaw Massacre*, *Poltergeist* was very scary with state-of-the-art special effects. Although it got mixed reviews, many Hollywood insiders predicted it would be Spielberg's biggest movie of the summer.

E.T. The Extra-Terrestrial was different. Although Spielberg was a famous director, *E.T.* was seen as a "softer" picture lacking the thrill of other movies he had directed like *Raiders of the Lost Ark* or *Jaws*. Besides, he had already made a movie about aliens: *Close Encounters of the Third Kind*. Movie experts believed *E.T. The Extra-Terrestrial* would only be a modest success. The experts were wrong.

The film about a homeless alien, lost and far from home, was an instant hit. The day it was released, many movie theaters reported longer lines and sold more tickets than they ever had before. Its message about love and compassion appealed to adults. College professors and religious scholars wrote about the film's spiritual themes: a superior being sent from the heavens, his death, and resurrection.

Teenagers flocked to the film, drawn by its humor and subversive story line about opposing authority—particularly the authority represented by the movie's cruel-hearted government agents.

Drew's mother, Jaid, was also an actor. She eventually became Drew's full-time manager. Problems developed between the two when Drew was still very young.

And yes, children loved *E.T. The Extra-Terrestrial*.

For a summer movie to become a blockbuster, it needs viewers who enjoy the movie enough to see it over and over. In 1982, some filmgoers saw *E.T. The Extra-Terrestrial* dozens of times. In two months, the movie grossed over $200 million in the United States alone. In an era when many movie theaters only had a single screen, some showed *E.T.* throughout the fall. It would go on to earn over $700 million worldwide, back when the average ticket price was about half of what it is today. It would be the top-grossing movie until well into the 1990s.

By the autumn of 1982, most newspapers and magazines had carried stories about the movie's director, its special effects, and its 10-year-old lead, Henry Thomas. Reporters began to focus their attention on the little girl who had "stolen the spotlight" from the film's loveable alien in every scene she was in. The phrase she'd come up with on her own, "Give me a break, Elliot," was one of the movie's best-known lines.

4

FAMILY HISTORY

T he day after *E.T. The Extra-Terrestrial*'s 1982 premiere, Drew Barrymore was in a Universal City, California, hotel lobby with costars Henry Thomas and Robert MacNaughton. Around her, whispers of "those are them, those are the kids from *E.T.*" could be heard, and Drew realized that her life was about to change.

Her role in the film enabled her to travel to premieres in Japan and across Europe. Everywhere she went, fans asked her for her autograph. Getting another job wasn't difficult. Because of the film's popularity, every director, casting director, and producer thought of her first when they were looking for a preteen actress. Across the country, much of the attention she received was based on one article, a profile in *People* magazine.

Getting profiled in *People* was a big deal for anyone, but for a girl who was still in first grade, it was enormous. The article described her interest in popular music and how much she loved working with Steven Spielberg.

The magazine's photographer posed young Drew in a shot similar to the famous "Great Profile" picture of her grandfather, John Barrymore. Like many articles to come, the piece described her ancestor's sordid history.

John Barrymore, Jr. is one in a long line of Hollywood Barrymores. As the most recent descendant in the Barrymore line, Drew was the heiress to a tragic story.

Although it is possible to succeed in Hollywood with few connections and an unknown last name, some of the best-known Hollywood professionals are members of families that have been in the business for generations. It isn't just actors, such as the Sheens, the Douglases, the Fondas. It's also the less well-known: the directors, the producers, the stunt performers, and the special effects artists.

Still, in all of Hollywood, there are few families as famous and as tragic as the Barrymores.

In the middle of the 19th century, Louisa Lane married Irish comedic actor, John Drew, who drank himself to death by age 34. Their daughter Georgie, who began on the stage at age 15, married Maurice Barrymore on New Year's Eve, 1876. The couple established themselves in New York, where both became famous for their work in the theater. Maurice, unfortunately, became even more well-known for his bad behavior off stage, which included heavy drinking and dating a number of women.

The two would have three children: Lionel, Ethel, and John. All would become actors, gaining their greatest fame from a late 19th-century invention—the motion picture.

Of the three, John Barrymore would become the best known. In the 1920s, his Shakespearean work led critics to call him the Hamlet of his generation. In 1932, he would sign a multimillion dollar contract for two years and 10 movies. The films he made in that period—including *Grand Hotel* and *Dinner at Eight*—were very successful. But despite the success, Barrymore would be divorced four times and drink constantly.

Within 10 years he couldn't get a job. He died at age 60 in 1942 with less than a dollar in his pocket. His son would lead a life with similar failures but fewer successes. Relying on a famous name and a handsome face, John Barrymore Jr. signed his first motion picture contract while still 16, and appeared in a number of films. But as Margot Peters notes in her book *The House of Barrymore*, "the less than box-office hits could not satisfy a young man so profoundly anxious and insecure." In the 1960s he had racked up a string of drug- and alcohol-related arrests, and by the time his daughter became internationally known for her role in *E.T.*, his only contact with her was to ask for money.

Around the time of *E.T. The Extra-Terrestrial*'s release, the hectic life Drew and Jaid had known was somewhat more serene. Jaid went out for fewer jobs. Mother and daughter were able to begin spending more time together. Despite Drew's growing fame, life was less stressful than it had ever been before.

The summer was approaching, and her year at the Fountain Day School was ending. On a pleasant June afternoon Drew's mother picked her up from school. Jaid asked Drew if she wanted this idyllic life to continue.

In her autobiography, *Little Girl Lost*, Drew remembered her mother saying, "We can go back to living our normal lives, with me working and you going to school and auditioning when I have the time to drive you. Or we can turn it all over to you and let you pursue your career."

The decision was an easy one. She loved having her mother around and she loved being an actress. So Drew kept looking for work and her mother became her manager, finding Drew acting jobs and handling her money and her publicity. Drew was still in first grade when she became the family breadwinner.

Not long after that significant discussion,

Drew was back on a set. She'd been cast as the star of the movie *Irreconcilable Differences*. Although every film set is like a family, Drew quickly learned some film sets are like families that don't get along.

Drew's role was a young girl trying to divorce her parents, played by Ryan O'Neal and Shelley Long. Because Drew was in nearly every scene, her hours were quite long. This was made even worse by the constant arguments over every take between the movie's producer and its director. Very simple scenes often required more than 30 takes to shoot.

Although *Irreconcilable Differences* wasn't successful, one scene became memorable for its eerie foreshadowing. During a New Year's Eve party, Drew's character sits alone, ignored by her father. Lonely and bored, she quickly downs two glasses of champagne. The scene would later be played out in real life.

When *Irreconcilable Differences* wrapped, Drew was tired and unhappy. After enduring so much on the set, she wasn't even sure if she wanted to continue acting. Her life away from the movie world changed as well. While much of Drew's money was put away, there was enough left over for Jaid to buy a two-bedroom house in Sherman Oaks, a tree-lined neighborhood in the San Fernando Valley section of Los Angeles.

Drew began attending second grade at the private Westland School. The problems she had at the new school were even worse than at the old one. Working in television or films wasn't unusual for kids at schools like Fountain Day or Westland. A number of them went on auditions regularly, landing parts in commercials along with small television and movie roles. However, having a leading role in the most popular movie in the United States meant Drew was singled out

for attention. Drew's classmates at Westland saw her only as a celebrity. They made her feel out of place and uncomfortable. The few kids who spoke to her were only interested in what it was like to be in *E.T.*

Although *Irreconcilable Differences* made her want to quit acting, her problems at the Westland School drew her back. When her mother described the script for the movie *Firestarter*, Drew was quickly interested. She already knew about the book and its author, Stephen King. She would portray a 10-year-old girl who could start fires just by thinking about them while being pursued by a shadowy government agency trying to kidnap her for her powers. The role would mean that once again, Drew would have a lead role with long hours and responsibility.

Members of the Barrymore family (pictured here) experienced more failures than successes in Hollywood. With her addictions spiraling out of control, Drew seemed to be on a similar path.

The movie was scheduled to be filmed at the Dino DeLaurentis production facility in Wilmington, North Carolina. This would mean Jaid and Drew would have to leave Los Angeles for several months. Moving to North Carolina gave Drew the chance to be part of a family again—not just the family of a movie set, but a real family as well.

During the production of *Firestarter*, Drew befriended her stand-in, Jennifer Ward. Stand-ins are hired for their resemblance to the actors and are utilized during lighting set ups, a process where the director of photography uses someone who matches the actor's height and general appearance to "stand-in" while lights and other equipment are positioned.

Jennifer Ward was an eight-year-old local girl who lived in Echo Park, a suburb of Wilmington. Jennifer's house was near the home rented for Drew and her mother during the production. Having a friend her own age and spending time with a family where the parents were still married and had dinner together every night was a new experience for Drew. She soon spent more time at the Ward house than the one she shared with Jaid.

Life on the set was also an improvement. There were few arguments and production progressed fairly smoothly. However, her hours were just as difficult. Like her role in *Irreconcilable Differences*, Drew was in most of the scenes. Her day began in early evening, where she was tutored for several hours before arriving on the set. Filming was from dusk until dawn; often Drew wouldn't get home until 6 or 7 A.M. She'd sleep all day, waking in the late afternoon. Drew was in second grade and she was already keeping rock-star hours.

Despite the difficult schedule, Drew enjoyed making *Firestarter*, especially working with top-notch actors like Martin Sheen and George

C. Scott. "George turned out to be a wonderful, friendly man, the kind of man who you want to hug a lot," Drew recalled in her autobiography. "Working with him you always knew where you stood. . . . Early on, he told me, 'Drew, just forget about the camera and do your job.'"

Drew considers that the best piece of advice she's received about acting, along with Spielberg's earlier admonition that she couldn't act her character, but instead need to *be* her character.

Besides cast and crew, Drew made another friend of best-selling author Stephen King. Despite the scary novels he wrote, in real life King was a kind and gentle man who was so charmed by the young star that he asked her if she would be in his next movie. Drew agreed, figuring she would hear about it again in a year or two, if at all.

Instead, the next day King handed her part of script which he had spent all night writing. Based on two short stories from his book *Night Shift* (which was not related to the film her mother had made earlier), it would be another starring part for Drew.

Although she read the script and loved it, Drew had one request—could she have at least a few days off? Drew was exhausted.

After the movie wrapped, nine-year-old Drew experienced her usual emotional letdown. Leaving a movie set was always like leaving a family, but this time it was even worse. There was a real family she had to leave—the Wards. As she remembers in her autobiography, saying goodbye was "one of the most difficult and emotional things I'd ever done in my life. I broke down and cried and pleaded with my mom to stay."

Of course they both realized that was impossible. Los Angeles was waiting.

5

A PERFECT LIFE

When Drew Barrymore was on a movie set, she felt special. She was admired by people twice her age. Her problems arrived when she wasn't working. Every day of school was an endurance test. Her teacher predicted she would wind up a failure. A small group of boys made her their special target and called her "fatso." Some even threw their textbooks at her. But instead of fighting back, Drew began to believe the insults. It took all her will not to run home crying every day. Drew wasn't working and she was miserable.

Although she was only in third grade, Drew already had discovered the temporary escape alcohol provided. At the *Firestarter* wrap party she imitated the scene from *Irreconcilable Differences*, and, on a bet, downed two glasses of champagne. It was the first time Drew drank. It was also the first time she passed out.

The warm envelope of alcohol created a safe place, even if it didn't last. When she couldn't find her own drinks, Drew began scavenging at parties and nightclubs, drinking the dregs of liquor left in glasses by the adults. A sip here and a sip there— before she knew it, she was getting drunk frequently.

Drinking's idleness was temporarily eliminated when Drew returned to Wilmington for the movie *Cat's Eye*, the

---

Drew was starting to find comfort in alcohol and boys like then-boyfriend Balthazar Getty.

35

film Stephen King wrote with Drew in mind. Filming began the summer after her third-grade year. Most of the *Firestarter* crew members returned for *Cat's Eye*, and once again Jennifer Ward was her stand-in. She had her family back.

The drinking was left behind in Los Angeles. During the filming of *Cat's Eye*, Jaid told *People* magazine, "Drew and I have talked about priorities, and to her, being professional is the most important thing." While on the set, Drew's focus and professionalism were superior to even those of most adults. The challenge was when *Cat's Eye* wrapped and she returned to Los Angeles.

There was only one other environment that mirrored the world of a movie set. At the bars and nightclubs she went to, the adults treated her as though she was special. Even better was the fact that there weren't any mean little boys there. Drew's favorite place was a small club owned by a friend of her mother. Located in the artists' community of Silverlake, near Hollywood, the club was the only place other than a movie set where Drew felt safe. She could snag a beer and drink it secretly inside the women's restroom.

After she and a friend began smoking cigarettes, Drew had another unhealthy way to deal with boredom. In the Silverlake nightclub, Drew could usually be found smoking with friends and watching the adults from a loft area off limits to other club-goers.

Drew then discovered another way to feel better about herself: boys. "Becoming intimate with a boy seemed to satisfy my craving for affection," Drew explained in her autobiography. "I was always searching for father figures in older men, particularly the ones I worked with. But kissing boys gave me a way to get closer than I'd ever dreamed. It made me feel so good. I became guy-crazy, an addiction in which I used boys to find love, affirmation, and self-worth. It was like that song, 'searching for love in all the wrong places.' "

There were few auditions and no jobs. She'd entered a transitional age, where she looked too young to play a teenager but too old to play a child. But Drew Barrymore had one thing going for her—she was still famous.

Although Jaid was with Drew at the clubs and the premieres they attended, the two usually separated after they arrived, with Jaid meeting friends and Drew roaming around looking for diversions.

"By this time, regardless of Drew's lack of work, we had entered into a world that hadn't existed for us before," Jaid recalled in Drew's autobiography. "In retrospect, I should have paid much more attention to my instincts and trusted Drew a lot less."

For Drew's 11th birthday, her mother reserved New York's Limelight nightclub. When Drew arrived, she was surrounded by friends and a number of celebrities. It was a surprise party many girls her age might have dreamed of, except for the fact that Drew couldn't enjoy it. Under her mother's watchful eye, Drew found it impossible to drink a beer or smoke a cigarette. By then, she could no longer have a good time without getting drunk. In fact, Drew was already tired of alcohol. She was ready to try something new.

The opportunity arrived after another night out. She was in a car driven by her friend Amy's mother. Jaid had left for home. Drew was in the rear seat when the familiar scent of marijuana smoke wafted back from the driver's side. It was something she had learned about in clubs and classrooms, but she had never tried it before.

Amy's mother was kind of a hippie. She didn't eat meat and her apartment was used as a crash pad for rock star "wannabes." She would have been shocked to discover Drew's affection for liquor and cigarettes, but felt that offering the 11-year-old girl a joint was perfectly acceptable. After all, marijuana was all natural.

On the ride home, Drew took the gold pipe from her friend's mother. By the time Drew reached Amy's apartment, she was completely stoned. When her mother dropped in, only Drew's acting skills convinced Jaid everything was okay.

Drew quickly became a "pothead." The drug was easier to get than beer and much easier to conceal. Marijuana helped Drew sleep and escape her problems. Besides, everyone—even the anti-drug lecturers—said marijuana wasn't physically addictive.

"However, what no one ever explained is that the way marijuana enables you to forget your problems is one-hundred-percent addictive," Drew said in her autobiography. "The drug itself may not be addictive, but if you've got things bothering you, as I did, you're going to get hooked on whatever helps you to shove them aside. And I was someone who had problems."

Drew's problems painted every corner of her life. She was struggling in school—barely getting "Cs" and "Ds" while suffering the abuse of certain boys. At home her relationship with Jaid had deteriorated to the point where they only communicated by screaming. The one place she had previously found escape—her career—was fading.

After months of unsuccessful auditions, Drew finally landed a job—the lead role in a Christmas movie, *Babes in Toyland*. It was television, which some film actors considered a step down, but it was still work. The special would be filmed in Munich, Germany, which meant that she would be able to leave Los Angeles.

Babes in Toyland was going to be a three-hour

movie. The four-month shoot would consume Drew's summer, and once again she managed to leave most of her problems behind.

Drew didn't party in Germany like she had in the States. Still, the clashes with Jaid continued. One huge battle erupted over Drew's desire to spend a weekend with rocker Rod Stewart and his band, who were touring Europe. She wasn't even 12, but he invited her to join his entourage. Although her mother refused to let her go, she allowed Drew to spend a night out with Stewart and his band.

Once filming began, Drew rarely drank. However, there was another familiar comfort available on the set. Michael was her 15-year-old costar, and he became Drew's first serious boyfriend. Although he was four years her senior, Drew kept up. On set rumors about their behavior were serious enough to find their way back to Jaid.

Because Drew had won more freedom, Jaid

Although Drew played innocent kids on screen, she would later take bad girl parts based on the media's portrayal of her addictions. Here she poses with her fellow castmates of the movie *Bad Girls*.

Drew in 1995 with another one of her high-profile boyfriends, Eric Erlandson from the band Hole.

wasn't around every day. The two didn't share meals—in fact, Drew shared as little as possible with her mother. When Jaid found out about her daughter's behavior, she asked Drew if there was anything she needed to know about boys. Drew said she knew all she needed to.

After filming ended, Drew endured the usual letdown. This time her reaction was different.

"I truly believe it was over that period that I decided being loaded was a new way of life for me," Drew recalled in *Little Girl Lost*. "My depressions were more frequent and deeper than ever before and getting loaded was the only way I could rise above those depths."

Drew considered suicide. Although she didn't follow through on her darker instincts, she poured her energy into getting wasted. Certainly her new school, Cal Prep, gave her every opportunity. She'd been to four schools in six years and, like many new kids, she had trouble making friends. At Cal Prep she didn't get along with kids her age.

There was one difference between Cal Prep and the other schools—seniors. Drew described them as "good kids gone bad," 17- and 18-year-olds who were accepting of the much younger Drew, because her fame allowed her access to experiences they had only imagined—bars and nightclubs.

Jaid was beginning to suspect the depths of her daughter's addictions. She caught Drew smoking and drinking several times. Drew's own distrust developed as she began to view Jaid more as a manager than a mother. To Drew, Jaid was someone who needed to "get a life" instead of spending her time focused on Drew's career.

A movie role made their already unraveling relationship even more tenuous. Drew had worked hard to earn a part in the film *See You in the Morning*. Starring Jeff Bridges and Farrah Fawcett, the role as their troubled daughter enduring the couple's divorce was familiar emotional terrain for Drew. She knew what it was like to have problems with your parents.

The job required a four-month stay in New York. Suddenly, for the first time, Drew didn't want to work. She asked Jaid why she should care about some dumb movie. Jaid was shocked by her daughter's attitude, but insisted Drew take the job.

The truth was that Drew didn't really care about leaving her friends or California weather. She was worried about leaving her drug supply.

6

RECOVERY

Drew Barrymore was such a talented actress she was able to convince her mother for several years that nothing was wrong. By the winter of 1988, that began to change.

See You in the Morning was a movie Drew did not want to make. Jaid had never forced Drew to work before, allowing the actress as much time off as she wanted. This time was different—Jaid made Drew take the job not for her career, but to escape LA's temptations. In New York City, Jaid thought Drew would be safe. She was wrong.

In January, mother and daughter moved into their usual suite in the posh Mayflower Hotel. Jaid loved coming to New York, enjoying many of the diversions the city offered—the theaters on Broadway, the uptown museums, and the shops and restaurants in the Village. Drew, however, didn't share her mother's enthusiasm.

Before January ended, Jaid purchased a two-bedroom condo on 68th and Broadway. Drew spent as little time there as possible, instead crashing at a friend's apartment on weekends. The girl, a teenage model, passed for 21, and although Drew was a month shy of 13, doormen at New

As Drew hit rock bottom, no one was sure if she would ever be able to work again. But one of her first successes after her recovery was the movie *The Wedding Singer* with comic Adam Sandler. The film is set during the '80s—the time when Drew was going through her downward spiral.

York's trendy nightclubs knew who she was. The pair rarely had a problem getting in.

Drew also found a boyfriend, Bobby. Academically focused and from a good home, Bobby was a top honors student at an elite prep-school who had earned early admission to New York University. The age difference between Bobby, a student in high school, and Drew, a girl in middle school, wasn't a problem. They both shared a common interest: alcohol and drugs.

Mother and daughter fought whenever they shared space, so Drew spent her free time away from home. She bought a pair of rollerskates to save money on subways and taxis. Her allowance went toward the bars and clubs.

Although Drew believes no one she worked with on the set suspected her "double-life," she was sullen, withdrawn, and at times hungover. She began missing so many hours of mandatory tutoring that she was forced to make up the time on Saturday mornings.

After filming ended, Drew returned to LA and a brand-new drug: cocaine. Drew was 13 and already self-conscious about her weight. She had earned the lead in a movie, *Far from Home*, and the film required her to appear in a bikini for several scenes. Feeling overweight and unattractive, Drew believed coke would help her lose weight. Drew's experience was similar to other young drug abusers. Younger people, whose bodies are still growing, often go from their first drink to full-blown addiction very quickly. "[My] addict mind told me, 'Well if smoking pot is cute, it'll also be cute to get the heavier stuff like cocaine,'" Drew said in an interview with *People* magazine. "What I did kept getting worse and worse, and I didn't care what anybody else thought."

As Drew recalled in her autobiography, "Coke was the right drug for me. Neat and quick, with no apparent after-effect, coke allowed me to soar above my depression and sadness, above all my problems. What I couldn't see is that it eventually makes you go crazy."

Drew's crazy moment arrived on a heavy night of partying. Drunk and stoned, she called up her mother and demanded she leave the house. Drew wanted to be by herself when she he got home. She didn't want to face her mother.

When Drew arrived home later that night, Jaid was still there, waiting up and worried. Drew was enraged. Not caring what her mother witnessed, Drew grabbed a beer from the refrigerator and shoved her way past Jaid, slamming her bedroom door. As she chugged the beer, she could hear her mother making a phone call.

Although she was drunk, panic cut through the alcohol. In her mind she imagined the police coming to her room, handcuffing her and taking her away. She pictured headlines and mugshots splashed across the morning newspapers.

Drew returned to the kitchen, hoping for one more beer before the cops hauled her away. She didn't get the chance. Instead, she froze as the doorknob slowly turned. Drew stood in the kitchen, beginning to cry. But it wasn't the police—it was her friend Chelsea and her mother.

And they weren't taking Drew to jail. They were taking her to the hospital, the same place that helped Chelsea get off drugs and alcohol. Drew didn't even fight."By that time, I could hardly walk or function," Drew admitted to *People*. "She and her mother pulled me into their car. 'Where are you taking me?' I asked.

They told me the hospital and I said, 'No prob.' As long as it wasn't jail. The last thing I wanted was to get caught in public in handcuffs."

The place Drew was taken, ASAP Family Treatment Center, is a private drug and alcohol rehabilitation clinic located in Van Nuys. Founded by Dave Lewis in 1979, ASAP Family Treatment Center's program was similar to many others. As a psychiatrist, Lewis dealt with addicted children and teenagers years before founding the center. At the center every day was heavily scheduled with intensive therapy sessions: individual, group, family.

Like Drew, most of ASAP's patients began abusing drugs at a very young age, usually drinking by the time they were eight years old and becoming regular users within three years. The average age of admission to the program was 15; at 13, Drew was once again ahead of her peers.

Because the media focuses on celebrities enrolling in drug and alcohol programs, it might seem like everyone who enters treatment, or "rehab," is famous. The reality is most people who go into rehab are ordinary men and women—some who are quite young—whose lives are slowly being destroyed by their addictions. The key to a program like ASAP's success was no one got special treatment.

On her first morning at ASAP, Drew was barely asleep an hour when the white glare of florescent lighting automatically kicked on at 7 A.M. In the windowless holding room, a tech shook Drew awake. That day she began to get sober, attending multiple therapy sessions and going through a variety of medical examinations.

Unfortunately, although treatment is supposed to be the same for everyone involved, Drew had a movie to make.

Drew needed to leave the hospital by July 10th to film *Far from Home* in Nevada. ASAP did something they'd never done before. They increased her therapy and provided a tech—a former patient—who would stay with Drew during the difficult shoot. Despite their best intentions, going against one of the core values of the program would prove to be a mistake. Betty Wyman, who managed Drew's treatment, recalled in *Little Girl Lost* that the actress and her mother "were treating this almost as if it were hotel ASAP."

Another scene from *The Wedding Singer*, which portrayed a very calm picture of the '80s when compared to what Drew was really going through during that time period.

Far from Home provided a mountain of challenges for Drew. The script required a bikini scene. Even more difficult was the general atmosphere on the set. Like the movie's title, the cast and crew were indeed far from home and they played as hard as they worked, treating any downtime as an excuse to party.

Drew was experiencing a state some addicts describe as "dry time." In an essay she later wrote as part of her recovery, Drew explained that "Dry time is when you continue to sit around the things you're trying to get away from, like drugs and alcohol, and your feelings are still very much involved."

When filming ended, Drew was supposed to return to treatment. Instead, she went to New York to audition for a play. Her mother figured a brief vacation in New York City would be a safe reward for Drew's sobriety. This turned out to be a bad idea.

Alone in the Manhattan condo, the pair returned to their old patterns and fought constantly over Drew's desire for freedom. Only a few days after their arrival in New York, Drew escaped. Stealing her mother's credit card, Drew met up with a friend and the two began a binge of coke, alcohol, and cross-country travel.

After flying to Los Angeles, the two young girls went back to Drew's house. Drew recalls in *People* that they "decided to take my mother's BMW to go out to dinner. Even though I'm 13, my driving is pretty good. After dinner I called my mother and told her in this sickeningly sweet tone of voice that I'd be home soon. 'That's it, I'm calling the cops,' she said."

Later that night Drew was alone in her bedroom, changing for a planned trip to Hawaii when a man and woman walked in. The two weren't cops. They were private agents hired by her mother. They handcuffed her and took her back to ASAP.

This time it was different; Drew was ready. She realized she couldn't keep spiraling further downward. Drew stopped treating the program like "hotel ASAP" and began to get sober.

7

Taking Contol

In many ways, Drew Barrymore's recovery wasn't any different from any other addict's recovery. There would be another relapse in the summer of 1989, and other periods when she wasn't sober. Still, a year before her third and final stay at ASAP in the winter of 1989, Drew received a reminder that she wasn't like everyone else in rehab.

A reporter from the supermarket tabloid the *National Enquirer* learned about Drew's battle with addiction. On January 3, 1989, the paper's cover featured a blazing headline: "E.T. Star in Cocaine & Booze Clinic—at 13! The Shocking Untold Story."

Before the article even appeared, Drew made a decision. As she recalled in the Chelsea House series "Overcoming Adversity,"

> Sometimes it's better not to respond to gossip. However, I decided that this wasn't one of those times. I think it took courage on my part. But I didn't want to be considered another Hollywood tragedy. That's the last thing I am. I'm a success. That's why I decided to tell my story. If I've learned anything, it's [that it is] always better to tell the truth. And by doing so, maybe it will help other kids not to end up like me.

Throughout her recovery, Drew showed her strength as a person. She would later show her strength as an actor—and in the movie *Charlie's Angels,* her strength as a superhero.

She contacted *People*, the magazine that had profiled her years before, when she was first struggling with being famous. Less than two weeks after the tabloid article's appearance, Drew's face was on the cover of *People*. Inside she admitted to her drinking and drug use.

The piece concluded with Drew saying, "I'm not psychic. But for today I can stay sober. I never want to go back to my old ways. I know that. That is my future. One day at a time. I'm Drew, and I'm an addict-alcoholic. I've been sober for three months, two weeks and five days, and I'm really proud of that."

While the *National Enquirer* article got some attention, most of the public found the admissions shocking. Still, since the response was not negative, Drew appeared in a television program about recovering from drugs and alcohol. She also decided to work with the *People* magazine reporter, Todd Gold, on a book.

When Drew's autobiography *Little Girl Lost* appeared in 1990, it didn't just tell her story. It informed thousands of teenagers about the realities of addictions and recovery. Writing the book was also part of the healing process for Drew. Unfortunately, while overcoming her addictions was difficult and time-consuming, convincing Hollywood she was ready to work again would be just as challenging.

Her mother would not be a part of the process. The deceptions, the acting out, and Drew's downward spiral were all linked to her relationship with her mother. While Drew made her own choices and took responsibility for her actions, going back to her mother's house after she completed her time at ASAP wouldn't be healthy. Instead, Drew moved in with musician David Crosby and his wife, Jan Dance. Crosby was a former addict who had embraced the philosophy of the recovery movement.

Drew gained legal adulthood, or emancipation, which meant she would have access to her own money and was allowed to sign contracts and work adult hours. Despite being ready for a renewed acting career, Drew didn't work as an actress for almost two years. During that time she lived off the money she had earned. She also worked as a doorperson at several nightclubs and at a coffee shop in Hollywood.

Child stars who are known for their wholesome, innocent qualities often have a difficult time making the transition to adult parts. Drew's solution was to seek out so-called "bad girl" roles, where she could play dangerous, sexy women. If the news of her drug and alcohol abuse contradicted the public's image of her, her first jobs after rehab completely shattered previous perceptions.

In 1992 she earned a role in the summer television series, *2000 Malibu Road*. Directed by Joel Schumacher, who'd made his name with the feature films *The Lost Boys* and *Flatliners*, the program was a short-lived cult favorite.

Following the series, Drew starred in *Poison Ivy*. Costarring Sara Gilbert from the hit television show *Roseanne*, Drew played Ivy, a girl who she described in *Interview* magazine as "the kind of girl who in reality you would *never* want to become, but maybe when you were younger you even knew a girl like Ivy who made you say, 'Why can't I be that free?'"

While the film received mixed reviews, Drew earned good publicity for the part. She also played the part of Amy Fisher in *The Amy Fisher Story*. Fisher gained world-wide attention when she shot the wife of her much older lover.

It wasn't just the roles that were earning Drew

respect. She was also getting respect for her hard-working, professional manner. And once again, Drew's off-screen behavior also began to get her attention. This time it wasn't because of her drug and alcohol use but because of her body, and the joy young Drew took in showing it off.

While only 17, Drew posed for well-known photographer Bruce Weber in a glossy layout for *Interview* magazine. Drew seemed comfortable in the shots, although she was topless in a number of them. A few years later, Drew posed for *Playboy* wearing even less. "When I'm 40, I'm going to get the biggest kick out of looking at that," she told *Time* magazine.

Drew's behavior seemed to be less about being sexy or shocking than celebrating a sense of freedom. Freedom was what she had wanted when she battled with her mother, and it was freedom that she mistakenly believed she had found in alcohol. As she moved into her twenties, Drew sought a different kind of freedom—the freedom to control the parts she took as an actress.

Although she was developing a successful career, she also found that many of the parts she was offered were similar. This is sometimes called typecasting—when actors are always seen as a specific type: bad girl, innocent, hero. To avoid typecasting, some actors and actresses form their own production companies. These companies find scripts for the stars that allow them to avoid typecasting. The companies then try to develop those scripts into movies.

In the late 1980s and early 1990s, many movie stars had their own production companies. Unfortunately, the only thing most of these companies were good at was losing money. They were more of a perk than anything else, like a trailer on a set or a personal trainer.

Despite her wild streak that still shows through as a twentysomething, Drew has proven she's a mature and professional actor. She's put together a winning production company, with the surprise success *Charlie's Angels* to her credit. Here she and fellow co-star Lucy Liu meet Prince Charles.

Drew didn't want some perk. She wanted to own an actual production company, one that made films. Just as Drew is a role model to many young actresses today, Drew also had her own role models, mainly Jodie Foster. Egg Productions, Foster's production company, developed a number of films that were praised by many movie critics.

"We wouldn't take a vanity deal," Drew told

Microsoft News. "The industry trend at the moment was that vanity deals were a joke . . . We knew that it might take us a year or two to get our feet off the ground, so we didn't want anyone footing the bill and feel ripped-off because we weren't delivering anything."

Instead of looking for a studio to provide financing, Drew started a production company with her own money. It was a risky move, but she believed it would force studios to take her seriously. Drew was only 19 when she founded Flower Films. Her first project, *Never Been Kissed*, was the story of a journalist posing as a high school student. Done for Fox Films Entertainment, it went on to earn $55 million dollars. In an interview with *Premiere* magazine, company president Bill Mechanic, said of the movie, "It needed a lot of work, and she had an active hand in everything—every music choice, the casting from top to bottom. And it was delivered on budget. From that alone, she brings more to the table than most producers do."

Drew also starred in *The Wedding Singer* along with former *Saturday Night Live* comedian Adam Sandler. Not only was the film successful at the box office, but many considered it to be Sandler's best work. In both films, Drew abandoned her bad girl persona to play the part of a sweet and innocent character. She continued this trend again with *Ever After*, an update of the Cinderella legend.

In the late 1990s, she began working on *Charlie's Angels*, a remake of the 1970s television show. There were three leading female roles. She chose to play Dylan—the bad girl. "I fancied it because I have just played so many nice girls and losers and girls who have never been kissed or barely know how to kiss or puritans or these

In July 2000, Drew married comic Tom Green. The two never actually dated, rather their relationship blossomed through off-the-wall jokes and working together.

valiant, pure-intentioned, rarely-make-a-mistake characters," Drew told *Rolling Stone* magazine.

Although there were many rumors in Hollywood about on-set fighting, and questions about whether audiences would accept a movie with three female leads (Drew was joined by actresses Cameron Diaz and Lucy Liu), the film debuted on November 5, 2000, at number one in the box office, earning over $40 million its first weekend. The film's success was not just a reflection on her as an actress, but also on her skills as a producer.

Drew's personal life was also improving. She had been estranged from her mother for a number of years; the relationship was further damaged when Jaid sold some of Drew's childhood clothing and toys on an Internet auction. Drew believed Jaid's biggest problem was her own desire for fame, and that her achievements were all connected to her daughter. Still, during the year *Charlie's Angels* filmed, mother and daughter began speaking to each other for the first time in years.

Her relationship with her mother wasn't Drew's only personal success in 2000—she also found a new love. Throughout the 1990s, Drew was involved in a series of relationships, including most notoriously a 51-day marriage to Jeremy Thomas, a 31-year-old Welsh bar owner who Drew believes married her for his green card and the right to work in the United States. Besides Thomas and Jamie Walters, Drew was in long-term relationships with actor-writer Luke Wilson and the guitarist from the band Hole, Eric Erlandson.

Tom Green was best known for his MTV comedy program when Drew called him in to audition for a part in *Charlie's Angels*. "I met him with his manager and my director," Drew told *Rolling Stone*. "It was all very civilized and respectful. I was 'Wow, if he would only ask me out.'"

Although Tom Green didn't ask for a date, their relationship developed during shooting for *Charlie's Angels*. The pair enjoyed joking about their wedding and even Drew's pregnancy, although neither was true. A planned ceremony during Green's appearance on *Saturday Night Live* didn't materialize.

The two finally got married in July 2001. Their life together wasn't all comedy and Hollywood glamour. In February of that same year,

Tom and Drew were asleep in her Beverly Hills home when a fire began in the attic. The two were awakened by Drew's dog, Flossie. The young actress believes the dog saved her life. She even set up an honorary trust for him, so that if anything should happen to her while he's alive, the dog will be well taken care of. And in December of 2001 Tom filed for divorce, ending their marriage after only six months together.

Drew Barrymore is approaching her late twenties, and is entering a new phase in her career by Hollywood's standards. She is no longer a child, and she has to seek roles that reflect her maturity as an actress. This age may be as challenging for Drew as when she was 10 and too old to play a child but too young to play a teen.

As a successful producer, Drew Barrymore is poised to handle that transition as she has all of the transitions in her life: with a little humor, a little edge, and never far from the public eye.

Firefighters look through the debris after a fire tore apart Drew and Tom's house. Their dog, Flossie, woke them in the middle of the night just as the fire began in their attic.

CHRONOLOGY

1975   Born Drew Blythe Barrymore on February 22 to Ildyko Jaid Mako and John Drew Barrymore Jr.

1976   Cast in her first commercial, for Gainesburgers.

1978   Cast in her first television movie, *Suddenly Love*, starring Cindy Williams.

1980   Earns role in her first feature film, *Altered States*, starring William Hurt.

1982   Gains international acclaim for her part in *E.T. The Extra-Terrestrial*.

1984   First starring film, *Firestarter*, is released; although filmed earlier, *Irreconcilable Differences* is released later the same year.

1985   Nominated for Golden Globe Award—Best Supporting Actress for part in *Irreconcilable Differences*.

1988   Admitted to the ASAP Family Treatment Center in Van Nuys for alcohol and drug abuse.

1990   Autobiography *Little Girl Lost* becomes a best-seller.

1994   Forms her own motion picture production company—Flower Films; marries Welsh bar owner Jeremy Thomas—divorces six weeks later.

2001   Marries comedic actor Tom Green; Beverly Hills home destroyed by fire. Green files for divorce six months later.

ACCOMPLISHMENTS

Television

1978	*Suddenly Love*
1980	*Bogie*
1985	*The Adventures of Conn Sawyer and Hucklemary Finn*
1986	*Babes in Toyland*
1987	*Conspiracy of Love*
1990	*15 and Getting Straight*
1992	*2000 Malibu Road* (series)
1993	*The Amy Fisher Story*
1998	*The Larry Sanders Show* (episodic—1998)

Films

1980	*Altered States*
1982	*E.T. The Extra-Terrestrial*
1984	*Firestarter* *Irreconcilable Differences*
1985	*Cat's Eye*
1989	*Far from Home* *See You in the Morning*
1992	*Guncrazy* *Poison Ivy*
1993	*Doppleganger: The Evil Within* *Wayne's World 2*
1994	*Bad Girls*
1995	*Boys on the Side* *Mad Love*
1996	*Everyone Says I Love You* *Scream*
1998	*Ever After* *Home Fires* *The Wedding Singer*
1999	*Never Been Kissed* (producer/actress)
2000	*Scream 3* (producer) *Charlie's Angels: The Movie* (producer/actress) *Titan A.E.* (voice only)
2001	*Riding in Cars With Boys* (producer/actress)

FURTHER READING

Aronson, Virginia. *Overcoming Adversity: Drew Barrymore*. Philadelphia: Chelsea House, 2000.

Barrymore, Drew, with Todd Gold. *Little Girl Lost*. New York: Pocket Books, 1990.

Peter, Margot. *The House of Barrymore*. New York: Knopf, 1990.

Zannos, Susan. *Real-Life Reader Biography: Drew Barrymore*. Bear, Delaware: Mitchell Lane, 2001.

Websites

www.celebritycd.com/Drew_Barrymore/ Index

www.famousnetwork.com/drew_barrymore

http://moviething.com.bios/drewbarrymore

www.rollingstone.com

ABOUT THE AUTHOR

JOHN BANKSTON was born in Boston, Massachusetts, and began publishing articles in newspapers and magazines while still a teenager. Since then, he has written over 200 articles and contributed chapters to books such as *Crimes of Passion* and *Death Row 2000*. He has recently written biographies on Mandy Moore, Jessica Simpson, and Jonas Salk. John lives in Los Angeles, California, and is pursuing a career in the entertainment industry. He has worked as a writer for the movies *Dot-Com* and the upcoming *Planetary Suicide*, which begins filming in 2002 and in which he has a supporting part. As an actor, John has appeared in episodes of *Sabrina the Teenage Witch*, *Charmed*, and *Get Real* and in the films *Boys and Girls* and *America So Beautiful*.

John is especially grateful to his parents, Jack and Mary Ellen, who took him to see *E.T. The Extra-Terrestrial* more than a half dozen times at the Nugget Movie Theatre in Hanover, New Hampshire, during the summer of 1982.

PHOTO CREDITS:

page

2: Associated Press, AP
6: Associated Press, AP
10: Associated Press, AP
12: © Corbis
18: Associated Press, AP
20: © Corbis
24: © Robin Platzer/Online USA/Getty

26: © Bettmann/Corbis
31: © Bettmann/Corbis
34: Getty Images
39: Getty Images
40: Associated Press, AP
42: © New Line Cinema/ Online USA/Getty Images

47: © New Line Cinema/ Online USA/Getty Images
50: © Darren Michaels/ Liaison/Newsmakers/ Online USA
55: Associated Press, AP
57: © PACHA/Corbis
59: Associated Press, AP

cover: © Mitchell Gerber/Corbis

INDEX